629.47
R

P9-DBP-953

DATE DUE

SPACECRAFT

The Rourke Guides are a series of scientific and technical books. All measurements are shown in the Metric System. This is the system the scientific community uses world wide. A small conversion chart below will help those not familiar with the system.

In addition, we, the publishers have listed European terminology with American equivalents.

Metric System Conversion Chart

Unit		U.S. Equivalent	
millimetre, millimeter	(mm)	.039	inch
centimetre, centimeter	(cm)	.39	inch
metre, meter	(m)	39.4	inches
kilometre, kilometer	(km)	.62	mile
gram	(g)	15.4	grains
kilogram	(kg)	2.2	pounds
litre, liter	(l)	1.05	quarts
cubic centimetre, centimeter	(cc)	.061	cubic inch
tonne, ton	(tn)	2000	pounds

Terminology Aid

colour	—	color	queued	—	lined up
tonne	—	ton	RPM	—	revolutions per minute
defence	—	defense	stabilise	—	stabilize
armour	—	armor	organise	—	organize
aeroplane	—	airplane	fulfil	—	fulfill
centre	—	center	customise	—	customize
calibre	—	caliber	£, pound	—	$2.00
favour	—	favor	honour	—	honor
manoeuvre	—	maneuver	valour	—	valor
programme	—	program	sledges	—	sleds
BHP	—	braking horse power	ploughshares	—	plowshares (blade of plow)
tyre	—	tire	invalided out	—	medical discharge
petrol	—	gasoline	labour	—	labor
neighbour	—	neighbor	odours	—	odor
harbour	—	harbor	fibres	—	fibers
practise	—	practice	neutralise	—	neutralize
amphitheatre	—	amphitheater			

Space
Shuttle

USA

Blairsville Junior High School
Blairsville, Pennsylvania

SPACECRAFT

8784

by Ian Ridpath
Illustrated by Ross Wardle

THE ROURKE CORPORATION
Windermere, Florida

©1982 The Rourke Corporation, Inc.

Published by Granada Publishing 1981
Copyright ©Granada

Published by The Rourke Corporation, Inc., P.O. Box 711,
Windermere, Florida 32786. Copyright ©1982 by The Rourke Corporation, Inc. All copyrights reserved. No part of this book may be
reproduced in any form without written permission from the
publisher. Printed in the United States of America.

Library of Congress Cataloging in Publication Data

Ridpath, Ian.
  Spacecraft.

  (Rourke guide)
  Includes index.
  Summary: An introduction to space vehicles including
rockets, the Space Shuttle, Spacelab, satellites, space
probes, Vostok, Mercury, Gemini, and Apollo.
  1. Space vehicles — Juvenile literature.   [1. Space
vehicles]   I. Wardle, Ross, ill.   II. Title.
III. Series.
TL793.R543   1982   629.47   82-9051
ISBN 0-86592-759-6   AACR2

Contents

Rocketing into Space   6
The Space Shuttle   16
Satellites   22
Space Probes   30
Man in Space   38
Man on the Moon   50
Stations in Space   52
Future – Fact or Fantasy   56

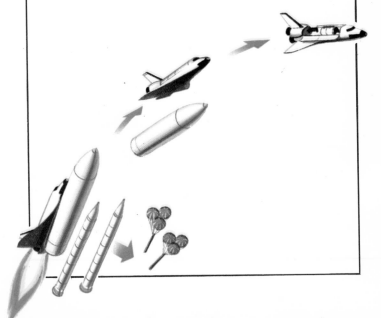

Rocketing into Space

Space begins as the Earth's atmosphere thins out far above our heads. Spacecraft, rocketed away from Earth to examine other parts of space, tell us a great deal about our own planet and our surroundings in space. Most satellites work automatically, but some craft have crews aboard to pilot them and to make observations. People can spend many weeks or months in space without ill effect. Manned spacecraft in the Apollo series have been sent to explore the Moon. In future, we should see manned bases set up in orbit around the Earth and on the surface of the Moon. There may also be manned missions to Mars.

Historic meeting in space. In 1975, an American Apollo spacecraft linked up in orbit with a Soviet Soyuz craft. An airlock, attached to the nose of Apollo, allowed the crews to move from one spacecraft to the other.

Saturn V Rocket

Lift Off!

Spacecraft separates

Stage 3 fires

Stage 2 fires

Stage 1 fires

To get into space we must break the hold of Earth's gravity. Imagine throwing a ball into the air. It rises upwards before falling back. If we throw it harder, it goes higher before coming down again. If we could throw it hard enough, it would go right around the world. It would be in orbit.

To send a satellite into orbit, we must push it at a speed of 8 km/sec. Rockets can travel at this speed and faster. A rocket moving at 11 km/sec will break away from the Earth completely, allowing us to send spacecraft beyond Earth's orbit to examine the mysteries of space. To achieve high enough speeds rockets are built in sections, known as stages.

To get back from orbit a satellite must be slowed down sufficiently for Earth's gravity to pull it down. All satellites are gradually slowed naturally over long periods of time by the thin outer gases of the atmosphere. But they can be slowed deliberately by firing a retro-rocket. When an object enters the Earth's atmosphere it gets very hot because of friction with the air. If the object is insulated with a heat shield, as are manned spacecraft, it can survive its re-entry. If not, it burns up in a ball of fire.

9

How Rockets Work

A rocket works by ejecting a stream of hot gas at high speed. The force of the gas escaping at the rear pushes the rocket along. By the same principle, an inflated balloon is pushed along as air escapes from it. To produce hot gases, rockets must burn fuel. The fuel can be either in liquid form, as it is in modern rockets, or it can be solid like the gunpowder in firework rockets. Typical liquid fuels are kerosene (similar to aircraft fuel) and liquid hydrogen.

Fuel cannot burn without oxygen. In space there is no air, so a rocket must carry its own oxygen with it. Liquid-fuel rockets carry liquid oxygen in a tank. Pumps drive the fuel and liquid oxygen from their tanks into the combustion chamber, where the fuel is burned. In solid-fuel rockets, the oxygen is mixed in with the fuel in chemical form.

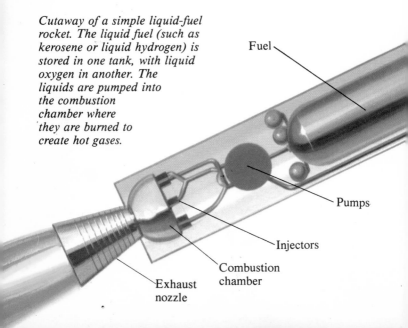

Cutaway of a simple liquid-fuel rocket. The liquid fuel (such as kerosene or liquid hydrogen) is stored in one tank, with liquid oxygen in another. The liquids are pumped into the combustion chamber where they are burned to create hot gases.

Fuel

Pumps

Injectors

Combustion chamber

Exhaust nozzle

Hot gases escaping at high speed from the combustion chamber create a force which pushes the rocket along in the opposite direction, just as the force of gas escaping from a balloon pushes it along. The Chinese firework-type rocket used in battle in the 13th century worked on the same principle.

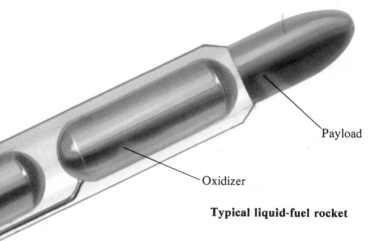

Payload

Oxidizer

Typical liquid-fuel rocket

Typical rockets have two or three stages. As each stage runs out of fuel, it drops away and the next stage takes over. This means that the rocket does not have to carry the unwanted dead weight of empty fuel tanks, and each successive stage can go faster as a result. In most cases, the stages are placed on top of each other; but some rockets have additional stages placed at their sides.

11

Rocket Pioneers

Firework-type rockets powered by gunpowder are believed to have been invented by the Chinese about 750 years ago. They used them for warfare, and the idea spread to other armies. In the 19th century, solid-fuel rockets were part of the armoury of British troops. But as artillery guns became bigger they fell into disuse.

◀ **Konstantin Tsiolkovsky** *(1857-1935), the Father of Astronautics. Early this century, before the first aircraft had flown, he wrote of using multi-stage rockets with liquid fuel to put satellites and space stations into orbit. But he was never able to build a rocket.*

Robert Goddard *(1882-1945)* ▶ *built and flew the world's first liquid-fuel rocket in 1926, although it only reached a height of 12.5 metres. By 1940 Goddard's rockets were soaring to 2 kilometres high at close to the speed of sound. But Goddard was never able to build the space rocket of which he dreamed.*

◀ **Wernher von Braun** *(1912-1977) designed the German army's V2 missile during World War II. After the war, von Braun and many of his rocket team went to the United States. There they helped build American space rockets, notably the Saturn V which sent men to the Moon.*

The first person to think of using rockets for space-flight was a Russian, Konstantin Tsiolkovsky. At the end of last century, he proved mathematically that multi-stage rockets could be used to travel in space, and he proposed the use of liquid fuels to power them. But he was only a theorist, and he never built any rockets of his own.

An American rocket pioneer, Robert Goddard, built and flew the world's first liquid-fuel rocket in 1926 at Worcester, Massachusetts. Goddard moved to Roswell, New Mexico, where he continued his experiments with liquid-fuel rockets until 1941.

In Germany, a rocket pioneer named Herman Oberth was also thinking and writing about space travel. He inspired young enthusiasts such as Wernher von Braun, who designed the German army's V2 rocket during World War II. Von Braun went to the United States, where he designed the Saturn V.

At a secret research base called Peenemunde on Germany's Baltic Sea coast, a German army rocket team led by Wernher von Braun designed the V2 missile, the forerunner of modern military and space rockets. Standing 14 metres tall, the V2 could carry a one-tonne bomb 300 kilometres. It first flew in 1942, but could not be put into operation in time to prevent Germany losing World War II. After the war, captured V2s were used for research.

V2 Rocket

Rocket Sizes

The size of a rocket depends on the size of the spacecraft to be launched and the distance it has to travel. The United States used Atlas missiles to launch men in its Mercury series, and Titan missiles for Gemini manned spacecraft. With additional stages, Atlas and Titan rockets are still used today for launching satellites and space probes.

The rockets used by the Soviet Union for its manned flights are based on the missile which launched Sputnik, the first satellite. Different upper stages are added depending on the mission. The upper stage used for Vostok manned flights was the same as that for the first Moon probes. A bigger upper stage is used for Soyuz manned flights. Soviet space stations and planetary probes are launched by a larger rocket, called Proton. Other nations are now joining in with space research,

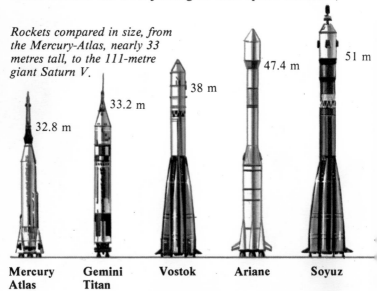

Rockets compared in size, from the Mercury-Atlas, nearly 33 metres tall, to the 111-metre giant Saturn V.

32.8 m

33.2 m

38 m

47.4 m

51 m

Mercury Atlas   **Gemini Titan**   **Vostok**   **Ariane**   **Soyuz**

including the European Space Agency which has its own rocket, Ariane. The giant Saturn V rockets were designed for the Apollo Moon project. The smaller Saturn IB was used for Apollo flights into orbit around the Earth, including missions to the Skylab space station and the Apollo-Soyuz link-up. Saturn V was the largest rocket ever built, but it and the Saturn IB are no longer used. All American manned launches are to be performed from now on by the Space Shuttle.

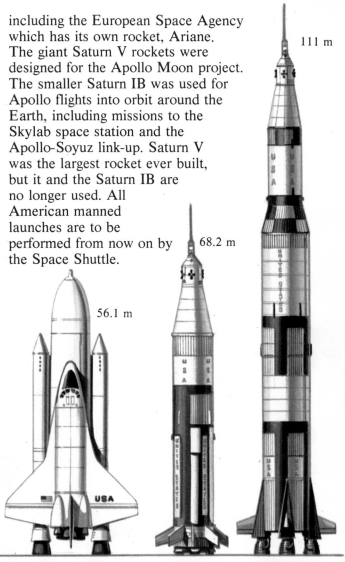

111 m

68.2 m

56.1 m

Space Shuttle   **Saturn IB**   **Saturn V**

The Space Shuttle

The Space Shuttle is a reusable space plane developed by the United States. It takes off like a rocket, but glides back to land on a runway like an aircraft. Because it is reusable, the Shuttle cuts the cost of space launches by up to 90 per cent. Previous rockets were destroyed each time they were used, and so a new rocket had to be built for each launch.

The Space Shuttle orbiter, the part that actually goes into space, is the size of a jet airliner, 37.2 metres long and with a wingspan of 23.8 metres. Most of its body consists of a cargo bay in which satellites are carried into orbit. Once in space, the doors of the cargo bay open up and the satellite is ejected. The Shuttle can also carry a manned workshop known as Spacelab, which will remain fixed in the cargo bay during flight. The Shuttle can carry up to 29 tonnes in its cargo bay. It also has the advantage that it can bring payloads back to Earth, thereby making it possible to retrieve old satellites or those that need repair.

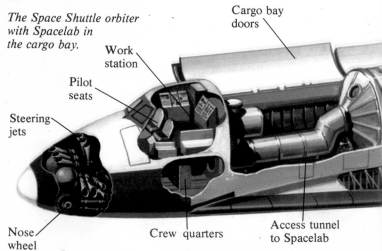

The Space Shuttle orbiter with Spacelab in the cargo bay.

Cargo bay doors

Work station

Pilot seats

Steering jets

Nose wheel

Crew quarters

Access tunnel to Spacelab

Astronauts pilot the Shuttle into orbit and back. They sit in a cockpit at the orbiter's nose, as in a normal aircraft. Scientists who will work aboard Spacelab also travel in this compartment during take-off and re-entry.

Anyone who wants to send a satellite into orbit can do so by booking it a passage aboard the Shuttle as though it were a normal cargo plane. By the end of the 1980s the Shuttle should replace nearly all American 'throw-away' rockets. American manned launches can now be made only by the Shuttle.

For astronomers one of the most exciting payloads for the Shuttle is the Space Telescope. This is a reflecting telescope with a mirror 2.4 metres in diameter, able to see the sky far more clearly from orbit than any telescope on Earth. The Space Telescope, plus other instruments that the Shuttle can carry, should tell scientists a great deal about the Universe.

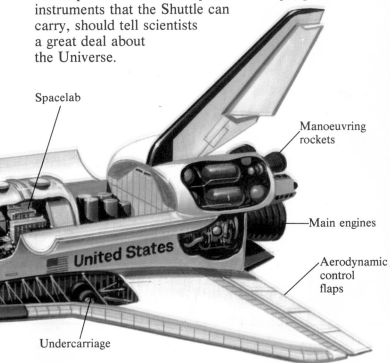

Spacelab

Manoeuvring rockets

Main engines

Aerodynamic control flaps

Undercarriage

Columbia Space Shuttle

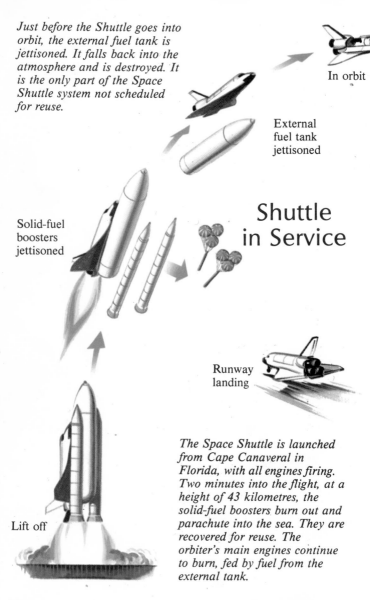

Just before the Shuttle goes into orbit, the external fuel tank is jettisoned. It falls back into the atmosphere and is destroyed. It is the only part of the Space Shuttle system not scheduled for reuse.

In orbit

External
fuel tank
jettisoned

Shuttle
in Service

Solid-fuel
boosters
jettisoned

Runway
landing

Lift off

The Space Shuttle is launched from Cape Canaveral in Florida, with all engines firing. Two minutes into the flight, at a height of 43 kilometres, the solid-fuel boosters burn out and parachute into the sea. They are recovered for reuse. The orbiter's main engines continue to burn, fed by fuel from the external tank.

18

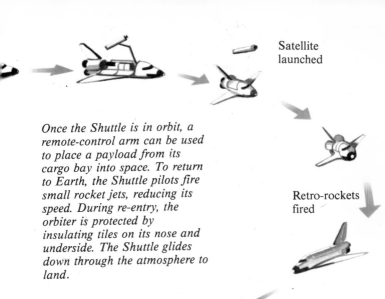

Satellite
launched

Retro-rockets
fired

Once the Shuttle is in orbit, a remote-control arm can be used to place a payload from its cargo bay into space. To return to Earth, the Shuttle pilots fire small rocket jets, reducing its speed. During re-entry, the orbiter is protected by insulating tiles on its nose and underside. The Shuttle glides down through the atmosphere to land.

Re-entry
to atmosphere

At take-off, the Space Shuttle is powered by its own engines, which are fuelled from a large tank attached to its belly, plus two solid-fuel booster rockets attached to the side of the tank. This combination makes the Shuttle the most powerful space launcher since the Saturn V. The solid-fuel boosters and the fuel tank drop away as the Shuttle climbs into orbit. When coming back to Earth, the Shuttle glides down through the atmosphere to land on a runway. After it has landed, it is taken to a hangar and prepared for its next launch. The Shuttle should be launched every month once it comes into full operation by the mid 1980s. There will be a fleet of four orbiters, each of which is expected to make at least 100 launches before needing replacement.

Laboratory in Space

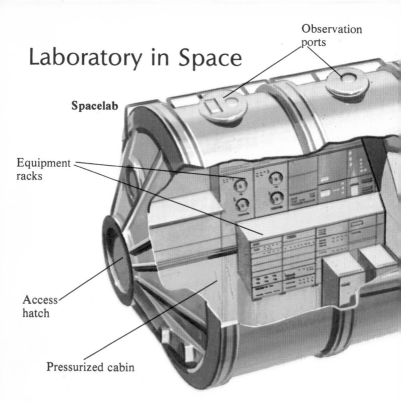

Observation ports

Spacelab

Equipment racks

Access hatch

Pressurized cabin

During the 1980s, men and women from the United States and Europe will work together in orbit aboard Spacelab, a space station built by the European Space Agency. Spacelab will be carried in the cargo bay of the Space Shuttle for missions lasting a week or more.

Imagine you are a scientist who has been chosen to fly aboard Spacelab. You will have undergone tests to ensure that you are fit, and you will have been trained for the mission. On launch day, you take your place in the nose of the Space Shuttle with six other colleagues. Three of these are professional astronauts who will actually pilot the Shuttle. You and the three other scientists will operate the scientific equipment on board.

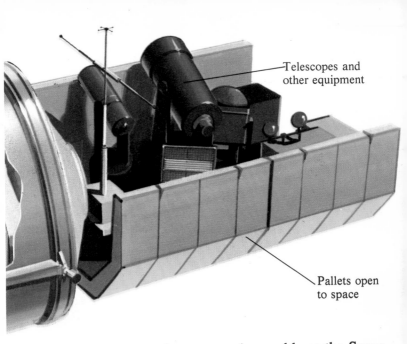

Telescopes and other equipment

Pallets open to space

Lift off! There is a roar and a rumble as the Space Shuttle's engines leap into life. You are off on your first trip into space. As the Shuttle ascends, you feel your body weight building up to three times its value on the ground – uncomfortable, but not painful. Ten minutes after launch you are in orbit, 200 kilometres up – and it feels as though the world has turned upside down! You float upwards in your seat as you become weightless. Unstrapping yourself, you can gently float into Spacelab to begin work.

When not working, you will live, eat and sleep in the crew quarters below the Shuttle's flight deck. After a week, your trip is over. You take your seat again as the Shuttle starts its descent back into Earth's atmosphere. The Shuttle glides down to land with a bump on the runway at Cape Canaveral. There is no hero's welcome, for by now spaceflight has become routine.

21

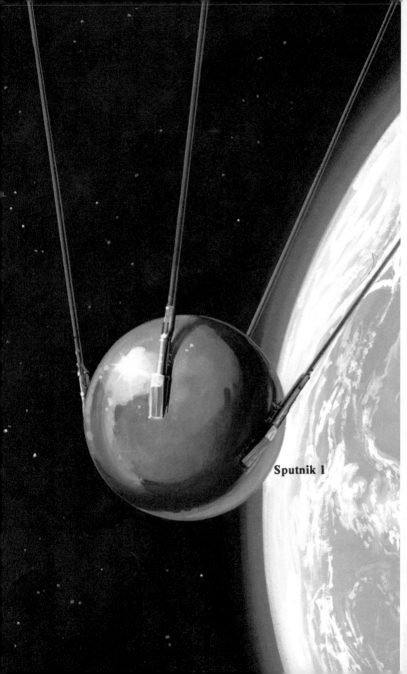

Sputnik 1

Sputnik 1, the first artificial Earth satellite, was a sphere 58 centimetres in diameter weighing 83.6 kilograms. It had four long aerials and contained a radio transmitter.

Satellites

On October 4, 1957, the Soviet Union launched the first satellite into orbit around the Earth. The satellite, called Sputnik I, caused a sensation in a world where space travel was still thought of as science fiction. Scientists on the ground tracked Sputnik by the radio bleeps it transmitted. Sputnik fell back to Earth after three months, having told scientists much about the upper atmosphere. Sputnik 2, launched on November 3, 1957, created even more interest for it carried the first living passenger into orbit – a dog named Laika.

After a series of embarrassing launch failures, caused by rocket explosions, the Americans put their first satellite into orbit on January 31, 1958. It was called Explorer 1. Smaller than the Sputniks, it stayed in orbit for 12 years. It discovered that the Earth was surrounded by zones of radiation which were named the Van Allen belts. A second US satellite followed in March 1958. Called Vanguard, it studied the gravitational field of the Earth.

After these American successes the Soviet Union leaped ahead again in the space race by launching more Sputniks containing dogs. These Sputnik launches were rehearsals for the first flight of a man in space, which came in 1961.

Watching the Earth

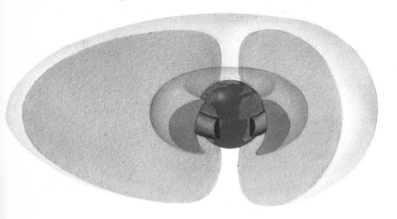

One of the earliest discoveries made by a satellite was that of the Van Allen belts, two invisible rings of radiation around the Earth. These rings are made up of atomic particles from the Sun which are trapped by the Earth's magnetic field. Before Explorer 1, the extent of the Earth's magnetic field was only guessed at.

Since then many discoveries about Earth have been made by satellites. The first weather satellites were an American series called Tiros, the first of which was launched on April 1, 1960. They were followed by improved satellites which returned better pictures and other information of use to meteorologists. Pictures showing clouds and storms help meteorologists to make more accurate weather forecasts. They give advance warning of hurricanes approaching land from the sea and of floods from the melting of heavy snows, thereby saving lives and property. Many other countries have now launched weather satellites of their own, which

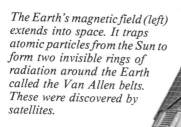

The Earth's magnetic field (left) extends into space. It traps atomic particles from the Sun to form two invisible rings of radiation around the Earth called the Van Allen belts. These were discovered by satellites.

Landsat

Landsat carries scanners to survey the Earth.

keep a constant worldwide watch on the weather. Eventually it may be possible to make accurate forecasts up to a week in advance.

Another valuable type of satellite, called Landsat, surveys the Earth's surface rather than its atmosphere. Landsats take pictures of the ground with special cameras. These pictures are then analysed by computers back on Earth, where they show up particular features of interest, such as rocks or vegetation.

Geologists use Landsat pictures to survey for areas where mineral deposits such as valuable metals or oil might be found. Landsat pictures are used to check on the growth of crops, for they can reveal areas where disease has struck. Landsat also monitors pollution in the air and oceans.

Some developing countries, such as Brazil with its vast rain forests, are making their first accurate maps from Landsat pictures.

25

Keeping in Touch

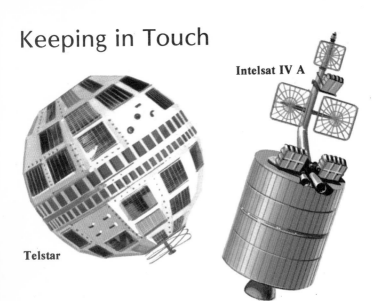

Intelsat IV A

Telstar

The most useful satellites of all are those used for communications. They flash TV pictures and telephone calls around the world in a fraction of a second. Messages are sent to and from communication satellites by ground stations. Each ground station has one or more dish-shaped radio aerials, like radio telescopes. The satellite amplifies the signals it receives before transmitting them back to Earth. Eventually, satellites will become so powerful that they will be able to broadcast TV signals direct to your home without need for large ground stations at all.

In 1962 the first live TV pictures were transmitted across the Atlantic Ocean between the United States and Europe via a satellite called Telstar. Telstar, and its successor known as Relay, orbited the Earth once about every three hours, which meant that the satellites were not in view of the ground stations all the time.

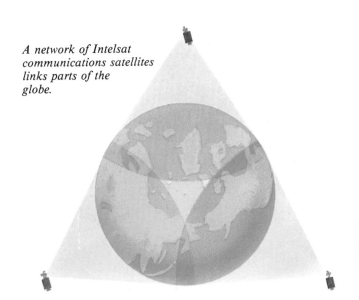

A network of Intelsat communications satellites links parts of the globe.

The solution was to put communications satellites in much higher orbits. At a height of 35,900 kilometres a satellite orbits once every 24 hours, so that if it is placed over the equator it appears to hang in the same position as the Earth turns. Such an orbit is known as a geostationary or synchronous orbit. A satellite at such a height is visible from one-third of the Earth. To go all the way around the world, a signal has to travel via more than one satellite. Most communications satellites are now placed in geostationary orbit.

A network of communications satellites called Intelsat now links the globe. Intelsat satellites are in geostationary orbit above the Atlantic, Pacific and Indian Oceans. The first Intelsat was Early Bird, launched in April 1965. It could carry 240 telephone calls or one TV channel. Since then, a whole series of Intelsats has been launched. The type known as Intelsat IV A can carry up to 9,000 telephone calls of 12 colour TV channels. Even bigger satellites, known as Intelsat Vs, are being launched during the 1980s to carry the world's booming telephone traffic. A number of countries have launched their own communications satellites to carry messages within their own country. Among them are the Soviet Union and the United States. A European communications satellite is planned for the 1980s.

Satellites for Good and Evil

Some satellites help navigators find their position on Earth. Navigation satellites transmit signals which can be picked up by ships and aircraft, allowing navigators to plot their positions more accurately than any other way. There is thus less chance of ships and planes colliding, and they can keep to their planned courses more easily.

Many satellites have been designed to explore the Earth's surroundings in space for scientific purposes. Astronomers have placed telescopes aboard satellites to study the Sun and the stars. Of particular interest are satellites designed to detect X rays, which are short-wavelength rays which do not pass through the atmosphere. These satellites have picked up X rays believed to be coming from black holes, mysterious objects whose gravity is so strong that anything that falls into them is crushed to destruction.

Satellites can also be used for military purposes. Satellites are regularly launched by the Soviet Union and the United States to spy on each other. Spy satellites have powerful cameras that can photograph vehicles and even people on the ground.

War in space? An artist's impression (right) shows how an enemy satellite might be zapped by a laser beam.

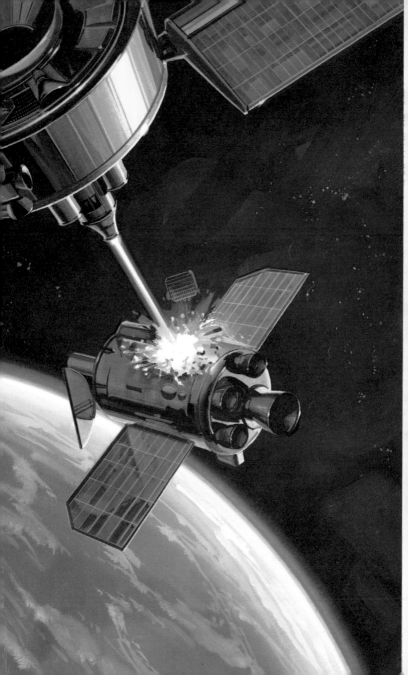

Lunar Orbiter

Surveyor 7

Space Probes

Before men set foot on the Moon, the United States sent several types of probe to survey it in detail. The first probes were called Ranger; in 1964 and 1965 a series of Rangers zoomed towards the Moon, photographing it in increasing detail before crashing to destruction on its surface.

In 1966 and 1967 five American Lunar Orbiter probes mapped the entire Moon from close range, spying out flat places on its surface where astronauts could land safely. Another series of probes, called

Lunokhod 2

Luna 13

Surveyor, automatically touched down on the lunar surface to give an astronaut's-eye view.

The Soviet Union has never sent men to the Moon, but they have sent robot explorers. Theirs was the first successful Moon probe, Luna 2, which hit the Moon in September 1959. In November 1970 the first of two Russian automatic Moon buggies, called Lunokhod, landed on the Moon. It was driven around on the lunar surface by remote control under radio command from Earth. Soviet probes have also scooped up samples of soil from the surface of the Moon and brought them back to Earth.

Probes to Venus and Mercury

Mercury and Venus are the two planets between the Earth and the Sun. Venus comes closer to Earth than any other planet – within 40 million kilometres.

The Soviet Union sent a number of probes which parachuted down through its atmosphere. They found that the atmosphere of Venus was unbreathable, being made almost entirely of carbon dioxide gas, which presses down with enough force to flatten a man. The temperature at the surface is like a furnace: 475° C. The clouds of Venus are made of droplets of strong sulphuric acid. Venus is one of the nastiest places imaginable. No astronaut could survive there, nor would he want to try.

A Soviet Venus probe parachutes down through the planet's dense atmosphere.

After passing Venus, Mariner 10 scans the cratered surface of Mercury.

Mercury is the closest planet to the Sun. It is also the second smallest planet (only the distant Pluto is smaller). Astronomers could never see Mercury clearly from Earth through their telescopes, and knew little about it until 1974 when the American space probe Mariner 10 flew past it. Mariner 10 showed that Mercury looked like the Moon, a rocky body with no air or water, and a surface covered with craters, caused by the impact of meteorites. The largest feature on Mercury is a round, lowland plain 1400 kilometres in diameter, evidently caused by a particularly large collision. There is no chance of finding any life on Mercury. Astronauts are unlikely to want to visit this planet.

33

Viking lander on the red sands of Mars.

Missions to Mars

Mars is the planet fourth in line from the Sun. It is about half the size of the Earth and is covered with red deserts. Astronomers thought that Mars might harbour simple plants such as moss. But space probes have shown Mars to be more hostile than expected. The air is too thin to breathe, and the temperature is colder than in the Antarctic. Parts of Mars are covered with craters similar to those on the Moon. The American Mariner 9 probe in

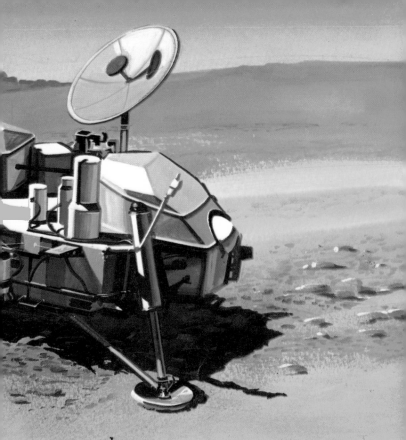

1971 photographed areas that looked as though they were once covered by lakes and rivers, although there is no liquid water on Mars today.

Two American Viking probes landed on Mars in 1976 to look for life. Their pictures showed rocks and sand dunes, but no plants or animals. One surprise was that the sky turned out to be pink, caused by fine dust particles floating in the atmosphere. The Vikings carried instruments to analyse the soil for any tiny life forms too small to be seen by the cameras. Alas, none was found; it seems that there is no life on Mars after all.

Journey to Jupiter and Saturn

Beyond Mars lie the giant planets, Jupiter and Saturn. These are swirling balls of gas. Jupiter, the largest planet of all, is 11 times the diameter of the Earth. Telescopes show that its atmosphere contains bands of colourful clouds, including a giant storm cloud three times the size of Earth known as the great red spot.

Spectacular pictures were received in 1979 from two American Voyager probes, which photographed not only Jupiter but also some of its moons in close-up.

After passing Jupiter, the Voyager probes flew on to the ringed planet Saturn, a smaller brother of Jupiter,

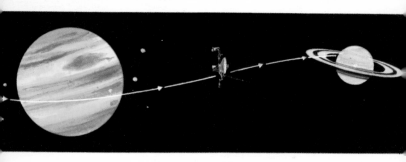

nine times the Earth's diameter. Voyager 1 gave astronomers their first good look at Saturn and its rings in 1980. The rings turned out to be much more complicated than expected, containing hundreds of ridges and grooves like a gramophone record. One of Saturn's moons, called Titan, is particularly mysterious for it has a thick, foggy atmosphere which hides the surface.

Voyager 2, which reached Saturn in 1981, will eventually reach the even more distant planet Uranus in 1986, and perhaps even remote Nepture in 1989.

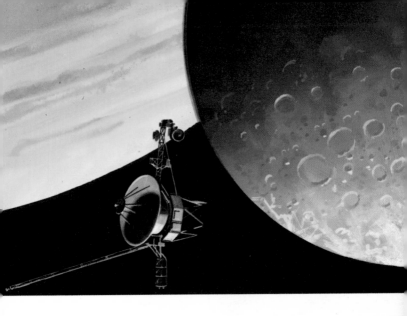

Voyager photographs Jupiter's moon Io (above). The pictures show active volcanoes spewing out orange and yellow clouds of sulphur. After passing Jupiter, the Voyager probe swings on (left) to Saturn and brushes past the planet's rings (below) revealing them to be much more complicated than expected, with hundreds of ridges and grooves. The rings consist of countless billions of ice-covered rocks about the size of bricks all orbiting the planet like tiny moons.

37

Man in Space

The astronaut in this picture is 'walking' in space. He is attached to his spacecraft by a cable along which air flows for him to breathe. In his hand is a jet gun which helps him to move around. Like all objects in space, he is weightless. He is moving around the Earth in orbit at the same speed as his spacecraft, so he does not fall behind.

A spacesuit is like a small personal spacecraft for the astronaut, keeping him alive in the vacuum of space while he is outside the spacecraft. Spacesuits for walking on the Moon had back packs which provided air, similar to the air supply in a diver's suit, so that astronauts could move around freely. When the astronaut gets back into his spacecraft he can take the spacesuit off.

A spacecraft is a cocoon in space, air-conditioned to keep the astronauts warm and to prevent them from suffocating. Electricity to power the equipment on board is supplied by batteries or by solar panels which collect the energy of sunlight.

Astronauts need to eat and drink while in space, but this is difficult in weightlessness. Drinks are squirted from a tube into the astronaut's mouth. Food is provided in several ways: in small bite-sized chunks which do not need cutting up; in the form of a paste which can be eaten with a spoon; or as a powder in a bag to which hot water is added to make soups and stews.

American astronaut Ed White 'walks' in space outside his Gemini 4 spacecraft in June 1965.

Vostok

The first person to fly in space was a Russian named Yuri Gagarin. On April 12, 1961, he made one orbit of the Earth in the spacecraft Vostok 1, landing safely after a flight lasting 108 minutes. Gagarin became a world hero. His historic flight created a sensation similar to that which followed the launch of the first Sputnik.

Vostok was a sphere 2.3 metres in diameter inside which the cosmonaut sat on an ejector seat. As the Vostok parachuted back to Earth after its flight, the cosmonaut ejected and landed separately. Unlike American manned spacecraft, which used to splash down in the sea, Soviet spacecraft touch down on land.

The launch of Vostok 1 meant the Americans were lagging in the space race, and the gap became even wider with the second Vostok flight, in August 1961. This lasted a full day, during which cosmonaut Herman Titov orbited the Earth 17 times. The United States began to catch up with its Mercury series of manned space-flights. But in August 1962 the Soviet Union leaped ahead again with a new space spectacular. They launched two Vostoks which orbited the Earth at the same time. One carried cosmonaut Andrian Nikolayev, and in the other was Pavel Popovich. In June 1963 came another twin Vostok launch, one of the craft carrying the first space woman, Valentina Tereshkova. She later married Vostok cosmonaut Nikolayev.

Vostok was later modified to make a craft called Voskhod, which could carry more than one man. In October 1964 a three-man crew flew for a day in Voskhod 1. During the Voskhod 2 flight in March 1965, Alexei Leonov crawled through a hatch to make the world's first space walk.

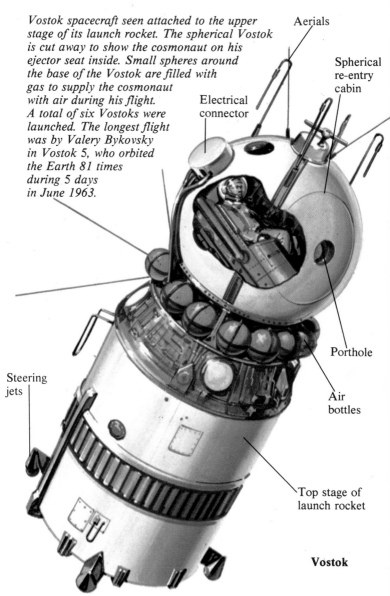

Vostok spacecraft seen attached to the upper stage of its launch rocket. The spherical Vostok is cut away to show the cosmonaut on his ejector seat inside. Small spheres around the base of the Vostok are filled with gas to supply the cosmonaut with air during his flight. A total of six Vostoks were launched. The longest flight was by Valery Bykovsky in Vostok 5, who orbited the Earth 81 times during 5 days in June 1963.

Aerials

Spherical re-entry cabin

Electrical connector

Porthole

Steering jets

Air bottles

Top stage of launch rocket

Vostok

Mercury

Mercury was a single-seat spacecraft in which the first American astronauts travelled into space. Unlike the spherical Vostok, Mercury was conical in shape, 2.9 metres long and 1.9 metres across the base. Being smaller than Vostok it was also lighter, 1.3 tonnes against 2.4 tonnes. Behind the astronaut was a heat shield, to which were attached the retro-rockets that brought the craft back to Earth. After being fired, the retro-rockets dropped away to expose the heat shield. The spacecraft re-entered blunt end first so that atmospheric drag would slow it down. Unlike Vostok spacemen, Mercury astronauts remained in their capsules until they splashed down in the ocean.

The first two manned Mercury flights, in May and July 1961, did not go into orbit. Instead, the capsule was launched by a Redstone rocket to the edge of the atmosphere before falling back again. During these so-called sub-orbital flights, which lasted a mere 15 minutes, the astronauts experienced the forces of take-off and re-entry, with a brief period of weightlessness between. Mercury missions into orbit were launched by the more powerful Atlas rocket.

The first American to orbit the Earth was John Glenn. On February 20, 1962, he circled the Earth three times in a flight lasting 5 hours. He was able to control his spacecraft while in orbit like a proper pilot, whereas Vostok cosmonauts were merely passengers in capsules which worked automatically.

Mercury flights became longer, ending in May 1963 with a 22-orbit flight by Gordon Cooper. But the achievements of Mercury could not match those of the Vostok flights, which showed that the Soviet Union was well ahead in the space race.

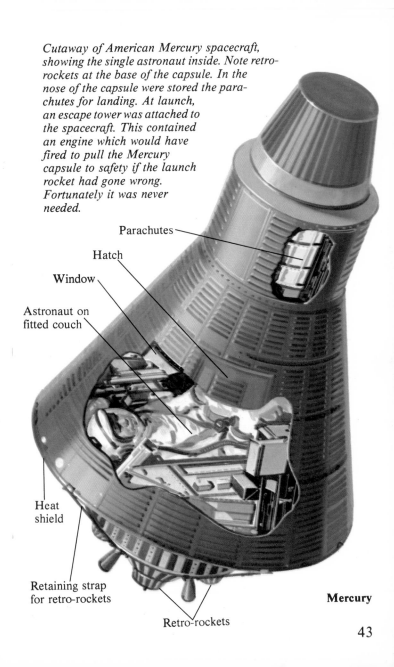

Cutaway of American Mercury spacecraft, showing the single astronaut inside. Note retro-rockets at the base of the capsule. In the nose of the capsule were stored the parachutes for landing. At launch, an escape tower was attached to the spacecraft. This contained an engine which would have fired to pull the Mercury capsule to safety if the launch rocket had gone wrong. Fortunately it was never needed.

Parachutes

Hatch

Window

Astronaut on fitted couch

Heat shield

Retaining strap for retro-rockets

Retro-rockets

Mercury

43

Gemini

Following the Mercury series of flights, the United States built a bigger and better manned spacecraft, capable of holding two astronauts. It was called Gemini. In Gemini spacecraft, American astronauts practised meeting and docking with other craft in orbit. Astronauts left their capsules to walk and work in space. All these techniques had to be perfected before the planned Apollo missions to the Moon could take place. The success of the Gemini series thrust the United States firmly into the lead in the space race.

Gemini came in two parts. The astronauts rode in the conical forward part of Gemini, sitting on ejector seats which would have shot them to safety if the launch rocket had gone wrong. Above them were hatches through which they could crawl to make space walks. This part of Gemini was 3.3 metres long and 2.3 metres across the base.

Behind the conical crew compartment was an equipment section which contained supplies of air and electrical power. It also housed the retro-rockets. This equipment section was discarded before re-entry to expose the heat shield at the base of the crew compartment.

Gemini was launched by the powerful two-stage Titan rocket. The first manned Gemini launch took place in March 1965. There followed nine more Gemini flights. On the second mission Ed White made the first American space walk. Another mission, commanded by Neil Armstrong (later to become the first man on the Moon), made the first-ever space docking. Other missions set endurance records of up to 14 days in orbit. The Gemini series had proved a great success by the time it finished in November 1966.

Gemini was the first manned spacecraft which could be moved from one orbit to another, to catch up with other craft and to dock with them. It was steered by small rocket jets in its nose and sides. Radar helped the astronauts locate and home in on their targets. On the control panel was a computer which kept track of where they were in space for navigation, docking and re-entry purposes. The equipment section included air tanks, power supplies and retro-rockets. The overall length of Gemini was 5.6 metres, and its total weight was about 3.5 tonnes.

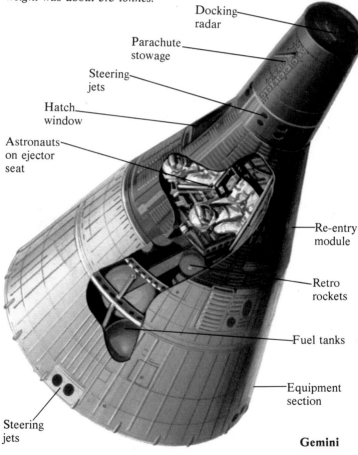

Docking radar

Parachute stowage

Steering jets

Hatch window

Astronauts on ejector seat

Re-entry module

Retro rockets

Fuel tanks

Equipment section

Steering jets

Gemini

45

Apollo

On May 25, 1961, six weeks after Yuri Gagarin's historic flight in Vostok 1, American President John Kennedy decided that the United States should try to land a man on the Moon before 1970. The space race had become the Moon race. Apollo was the spacecraft which America hoped would win the Moon race, building on the experience gained with Mercury and Gemini.

Three astronauts sat in Apollo's conical command module, 3.8 metres high and 3.9 metres at its widest. The command module was their home in space while they travelled to the Moon and back. Behind the command module was the cylindrical service module, 7.5 metres long and 3.9 metres in diameter. This supplied air, water and electricity to the command module. It also contained a large rocket engine. This was used for putting the spacecraft into orbit around the Moon and for sending it back home again, as well as for any course corrections on the way. Smaller jets around the service module were used to make minor manoeuvres, such as when Apollo docked with its lunar module. The lunar module was the spidery craft which actually touched down on the Moon. Two astronauts crawled through a hatch in the nose of the command module to get into the lunar module.

Apollo successfully met President Kennedy's challenge. The craft was launched to the Moon by the world's most powerful rocket, the Saturn V, specially designed for the purpose. Apollo craft also ferried three crews to America's Skylab space station in 1973. For such launches into Earth orbit, not requiring the lunar module, the smaller Saturn IB rocket was used. The last Apollo flight linked up with a Soviet Soyuz in 1975.

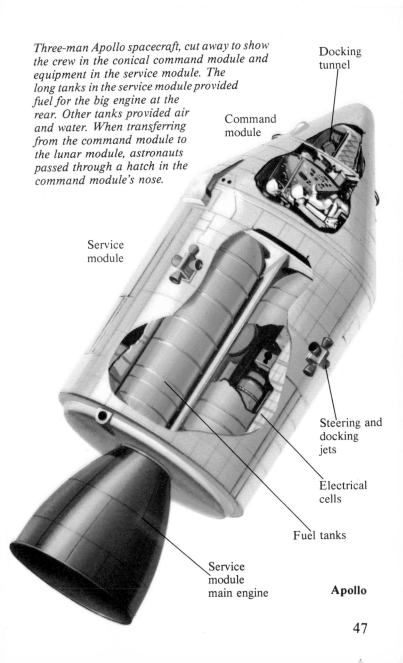

Three-man Apollo spacecraft, cut away to show the crew in the conical command module and equipment in the service module. The long tanks in the service module provided fuel for the big engine at the rear. Other tanks provided air and water. When transferring from the command module to the lunar module, astronauts passed through a hatch in the command module's nose.

Docking tunnel

Command module

Service module

Steering and docking jets

Electrical cells

Fuel tanks

Service module main engine

Apollo

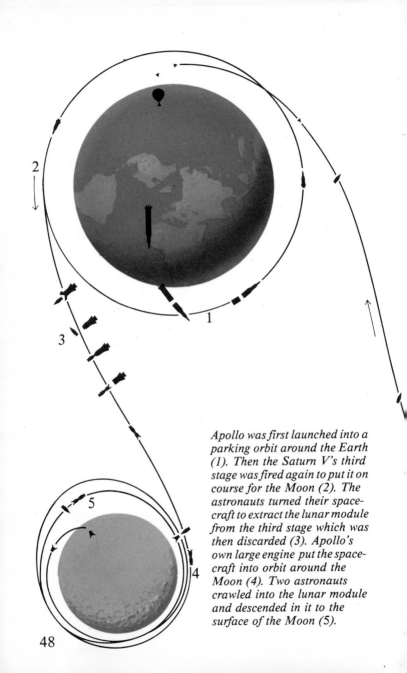

Apollo was first launched into a parking orbit around the Earth (1). Then the Saturn V's third stage was fired again to put it on course for the Moon (2). The astronauts turned their spacecraft to extract the lunar module from the third stage which was then discarded (3). Apollo's own large engine put the spacecraft into orbit around the Moon (4). Two astronauts crawled into the lunar module and descended in it to the surface of the Moon (5).

48

Reach for the Moon

Apollo astronauts used the lunar module to land on the Moon. At launch, this was stored underneath the command and service modules. Once safely on the way to the Moon, the astronauts turned their command and service modules to dock with the lunar module and extract it from the top stage of the launch rocket. The lunar module was a two-stage craft, standing seven metres tall. The two astronauts who were to make the Moon landing travelled in the top stage. The four-legged bottom half contained a large engine for controlling the descent and touch-down on the Moon. The astronauts climbed down to the lunar surface by a ladder. When their exploration was finished, the astronauts blasted off from the Moon in the top stage of the lunar module, using the lower half as a launch pad. They docked with their third companion who had been orbiting the Moon in the mother ship. Finally, the top stage of the lunar module was abandoned before the journey home. All the stages of the Moon mission were carefully rehearsed in space before the first manned Moon landing was attempted.

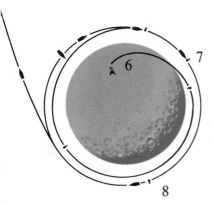

The two astronauts blasted off from the Moon in the top half of the lunar module (6). They linked up with the Apollo mother ship (7), which then set course for Earth, after dropping the lunar module (8).

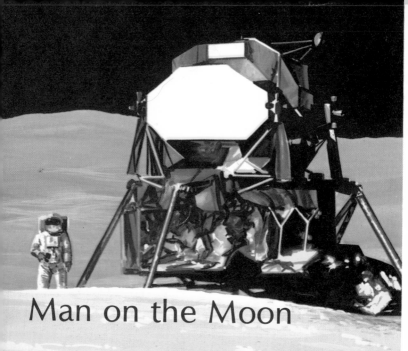

Man on the Moon

On July 20, 1969, the lunar module of Apollo 11 touched down on one of the Moon's flat lowland plains known as the Sea of Tranquility. (The name was given by astronomers long ago before it was realised that there is no water on the Moon.) Astronaut Neil Armstrong, commander of Apollo 11, climbed down the ladder of the lunar module and stepped onto the Moon. He said: 'That's one small step for a man; one giant leap for mankind.' He was joined on the surface by Edwin Aldrin. The two men set up experiments and collected samples of lunar rock before taking off to rejoin Michael Collins in the command module orbiting above.

A total of six Apollo crews visited the surface of the Moon. One landing, that of Apollo 13, had to be cancelled after an explosion damaged the service

After touching down in their lunar module, the Apollo astronauts tried out their electric-powered Moon buggy.

module; the astronauts were lucky enough to return to Earth alive. From Apollo 15 onwards, an electric-powered Moon car was carried in the lunar module. This allowed astronauts to explore much wider areas of the Moon. The last lunar landing mission, Apollo 17 in December 1972, was the longest of all. Astronauts Eugene Cernan and Harrison Schmitt remained on the Moon for 75 hours, during which they drove 35 kilometres in their lunar rover.

The Apollo missions brought back a total of 365 kilograms of lunar samples, and provided scientists with extensive information about the history of the Moon. At present, the United States has no plans to return to the Moon. But the Russians may try to set up bases there in a few years' time.

Stations in Space

Skylab was an American space station, made from the converted top stage of a Saturn V rocket. It was 36 metres long and weighed 75 tonnes, making it the biggest and heaviest object ever launched. It was put into orbit around the Earth on May 14, 1973. But during the launch it was damaged. One of the wing-like solar panels which generate electricity was torn off, as was a shield to protect the craft from meteorites that might crash into it.

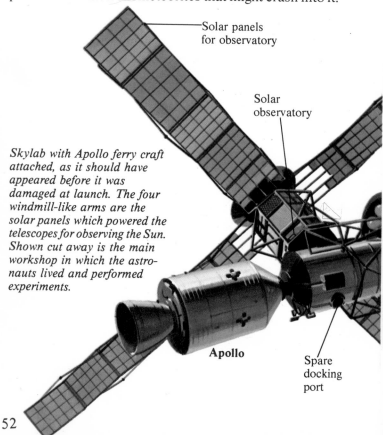

Solar panels
for observatory

Solar
observatory

Skylab with Apollo ferry craft attached, as it should have appeared before it was damaged at launch. The four windmill-like arms are the solar panels which powered the telescopes for observing the Sun. Shown cut away is the main workshop in which the astronauts lived and performed experiments.

Apollo

Spare
docking
port

The first Skylab crew, who were ferried up in an Apollo capsule, had to repair the station before they could begin their month aboard. Two other crews followed, the last crew remaining aboard Skylab for 84 days.

Aboard Skylab, the crews made observations of the Earth and Sun. They also experimented with making new forms of glass and metal alloys. Substances which do not mix properly under the pull of Earth's gravity can be made to mix in weightlessness. The production of a new material in this way could form the basis of space industries.

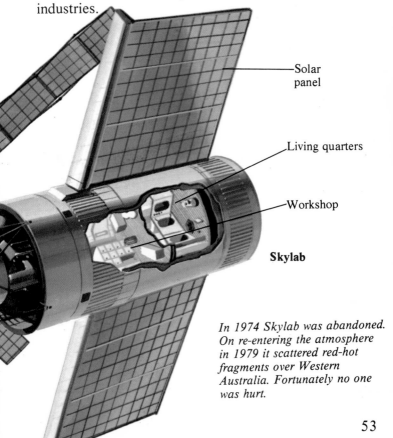

Solar panel

Living quarters

Workshop

Skylab

In 1974 Skylab was abandoned. On re-entering the atmosphere in 1979 it scattered red-hot fragments over Western Australia. Fortunately no one was hurt.

Salyut

In 1971, the Soviet Union launched its first space station, Salyut 1. There followed a whole series of Salyuts, in which cosmonauts made marathon space-flights. Salyut is the converted top stage of a Proton rocket. It is 12 metres long and 4 metres across at its widest; it weighs 18.5 tonnes. Salyut has only one-quarter the room of the American Skylab.

Cosmonauts are ferried to and from Salyut in Soyuz spacecraft. Soyuz has three parts: a cylindrical equipment section, which houses a main engine and power supplies; a bell-shaped crew section; and a spherical work compartment at the front.

Soyuz has had an unlucky history. On its maiden flight in April 1967, Soyuz 1 crashed, killing the one man aboard. It was redesigned and there followed a number of test flights during which Soyuz craft approached and docked with each other, as in the American Gemini missions.

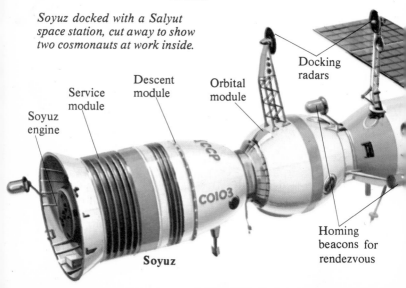

Soyuz docked with a Salyut space station, cut away to show two cosmonauts at work inside.

Docking radars

Descent module

Orbital module

Service module

Soyuz engine

Homing beacons for rendezvous

Soyuz

In June 1971 Soyuz 11, with a three-man crew, docked with Salyut 1 for a three-week mission. But air escaped from the Soyuz during its return to Earth, and the crew were killed. Again, Soyuz was redesigned.

Soyuz crews have made increasingly long space flights aboard Salyut space stations. In 1980, two cosmonauts stayed aboard Salyut 6 for a record-breaking 185 days. During these marathon missions the space station is resupplied by unmanned tanker craft called Progress, based on Soyuz. Other crews, including cosmonauts from countries outside the Soviet Union, pay short visits.

In future, the Soviet Union is expected to launch larger space stations and to keep them permanently occupied. Eventually, Salyut stations may be put into orbit around the Moon, and they may even form the basis of a manned expedition to Mars.

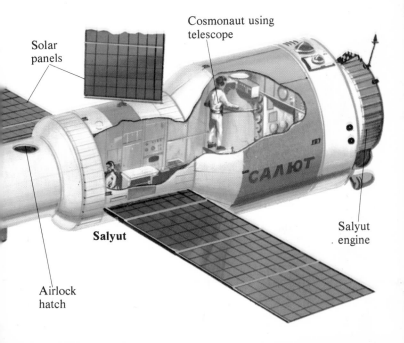

Solar panels

Cosmonaut using telescope

Salyut

САЛЮТ

Salyut engine

Airlock hatch

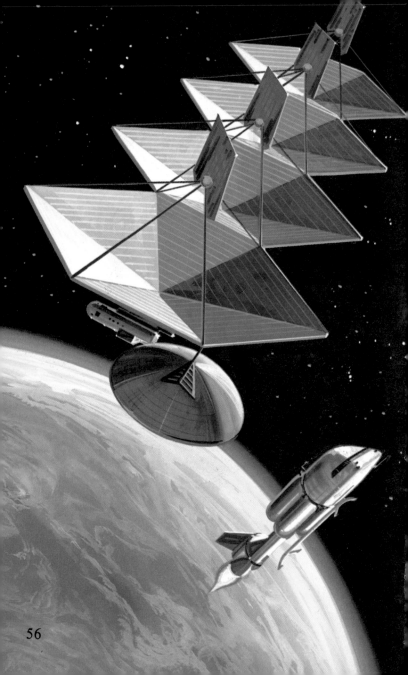

Future – Fact or Fantasy

In future, space will be used in many new ways to benefit mankind. One exciting possibility is for satellite power stations to help solve the energy crisis. These power satellites would be built in geostationary orbit around Earth. Out in space they would receive sunshine continuously, and would beam the Sun's energy back to Earth in the form of short-wavelength radio waves, known as microwaves. On Earth, the power beams would be collected by large receiving panels and converted into electricity. One power satellite could deliver as much as 10,000 megawatts, equal to the output of 10 large generating stations.

Another likely prospect is a base on the Moon where scientists can live and work, observing the sky and studying the Moon itself. Such bases would probably be buried underground, like scientific bases in Antarctica. The people on the Moon might also be able to mine the Moon's crust for the valuable metals it contains.

An artist's impression of a satellite power station (left) collecting solar energy in space and beaming it back to a receiving panel on Earth (below).

57

Living in Space

Huge space colonies, capable of housing thousands of people, could be set up in orbit around the Earth next century. They might be shaped like wheels, spinning to provide artificial gravity inside. They would be filled with air and the climate would be controlled so that people could walk around as freely as on Earth. Humans could spend their entire lives in these mini worlds in the sky.

Such space colonies would be built from materials mined from the surface of the Moon. Moon rocks contain valuable metals such as titanium, aluminium and iron, all of which could be used for building. The insides of the colonies could be landscaped to provide parks, gardens and lakes just like on Earth. All energy would be provided by sunlight, and the colonies would grow their own food in greenhouses.

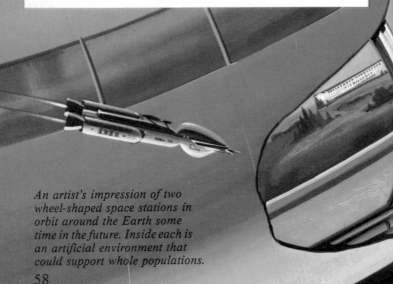

An artist's impression of two wheel-shaped space stations in orbit around the Earth some time in the future. Inside each is an artificial environment that could support whole populations.

To the Stars?

Next century, we might send our first probes to the stars. The stars are so far away that even the biggest of our existing rockets would take nearly 100,000 years to get to the nearest star. To send probes to the stars we need to build more powerful rockets that can go faster. These rockets will be propelled by nuclear power. One design is for a two-stage craft that gets its energy from the explosion of small hydrogen bombs. The force of each blast would push the craft along until it was moving at nearly 150 million km/h. Such a high-speed probe could reach the nearest stars in less than 50 years. When it reached the star it would radio back its findings to Earth, telling scientists about the star and any planets it might have.

Humans may one day travel to the stars. They might go in space colonies which will provide them with a ready-made home once they reach their destination. But such migrations to other stars will not happen for many centuries yet.

A nuclear-powered probe of the future heads away from the solar system to another star.

Index

Aldrin, Edwin 50
Apollo 7, 46-51
    ferry craft 52
    mission to moon 46-51
    Soyuz link up 15, 46, 47
Ariane 14, 15
Armstrong, Neil 44, 50
Astronaut 38, 39
Atlas missile 14
Atlas rocket 14, 42

Black hole 28
Bykovsky, Valery 41

Cernan, Eugene 51
Collins, Michael 50
Colony in space 58
Columbia See Space Shuttle
Combustion chamber 10
Communications, satellite 26
Cooper, Gordon 42
Cosmonaut 40

Dog, in space 23
Docking 44

Early Bird satellite 27
Escape velocity 9
Explorer 1 23, 24

Fuel 10, 11
Firework rocket 11, 12
Food, in space 39

Gagarin, Yuri 40, 46

Gemini/Titan rocket 14
Gemini spacecraft 14, 39, 44, 45
Geological survey, by satellite 25
Geostationary orbit 27
Glenn, John 42
Goddard, Robert 12, 13
Ground Station 26
Gunpowder 12

Heat shield 9, 43, 44
Hydrogen, liquid 10

Intelsat 26-28
Io, moon of Jupiter 37

Jupiter, probe to 36, 37

Kennedy, John 46
Kerosene 10

Laika 23
Landing, hard 40
    soft 42
Landsat 25
Leonov, Alexei 40
Life, search for on Mars 34
Liquid fuel 10, 11
Liquid fuel rocket, first 13
Living, in space 39
Luna probe 30, 31
Lunar module 50, 51
Lunar Orbiter probe 30, 31
Lunokhod 31

Magnetic field, Earth's 24
Man in space 22, 38-55
Mariner probe 33, 34
Mars 34, 35
Mercury/Atlas rocket 14
Mercury (planet) 33
Mercury, probes to 32, 33
Mercury spacecraft 14, 39, 42, 43
Meteorological satellite 24
Moon buggy 31, 51
Moon, missions to 49-51
Moon, survey of 30, 33

Navigation, aided by satellite 28
Neptune 36
Nikolayev, Andrian 40
Nuclear-powered probe 60

Orbital velocity 9
Oberth, Herman 13

Planets, probes to 32-37
Popovich, Pavel 40
Power station, in space 56
Propellant, rocket 10
Proton rocket 14
    converted 54

Ranger probe 30
Redstone rocket 42
Re-entry 9, 42
Relay satellite 26
Retro rocket 9
Robot explorer 30, 31
Rocket 9-15
    military use of 12, 13
    sizes of 14, 15
    Soviet launcher 14

Salyut 54, 55
Satellite 22-29

Saturn IB rocket 15, 46
Saturn V rocket 8, 15, 46
    converted top 52
Saturn, probe to 36, 37
Schmitt, Harrison 51
Scientific research 53, 57
    by satellite 28
Sea of Tranquility 50
Shuttle See Space Shuttle
Skylab space station 46, 52, 53
Solar panel 52, 53
Solar power 56
Solid fuel rocket 10, 11
Soyuz spacecraft 7, 54
    launch rocket 14
Space colony 58, 59
Spacelab 16, 17, 20, 21
Space probe 30-37
Space Shuttle 15, 16-21
Space station 52-55
Spacesuit 38, 39
Space Telescope 17
Space walk 38-40, 44
Splashdown 42
Sputnik 40, 22, 23
Spy satellite 28
Stage, of rocket 9, 11
Surveyor probe 30, 31
Surveying, by satellite 25
Synchronous orbit 27

Telephone, signals by satellite 26
Telescope, aboard satellite 28
Telescope, Space 17
Television, transmission by satellite 26-28
Tereshkova, Valentina 40
Tiros 24
Titan, moon of Saturn 36
Titan rocket 14, 44
Titov, Herman 40
Tsiolkovsky, Konstantin 12, 13

Uranus, probe to 36

V2 Rocket 13
Van Allen belt 23-25
Vanguard 23
Venus 32
    probes to 32
Viking probe 34, 35
Von Braun, Wernher 12, 13
Voskhod spacecraft 40
Vostok, spacecraft 40, 41
    launch rocket 14
Voyager probe 36, 37

Weather satellite 24
Weightlessness 39, 42
White, Ed 39, 44
World War II, use of rockets in
    13

X-rays, detected by satellite 28

The picture on page 4 opposite the title shows the burst of flame from the Space Shuttle's powerful engines as it lifts off from Cape Canaveral in Florida.